G000141614

IMAGINE

how we can reach the UK

Mark Greene
The London Institute for
Contemporary Christianity

Authentic

Cover design by 4-9-0 ltd.
Photography by Adam Greene, tel 02392 655 657
email: adamgreene@tiscali.co.uk

Print Management by Adare Carwin

CONTENTS

Mark Greene used to work in advertising and is prepared to admit it. He is now the Director of the London Institute for Contemporary Christianity which focuses on helping Christians live and share their faith in the contemporary world. Before that he was Vice-Principal and Lecturer in Communications at London Bible College. Mark writes and speaks widely on workplace ministry, contemporary culture and media.

Mark is married to Katriina, a Finn, and they have three exuberant children Matti, Tomas and Anna-Marie, and an even more exuberant dog called Spark.

FOREWORD

In February of 2003 the Evangelical Alliance did something we have never done before – we gave over our entire magazine to one issue and one writer, a writer who wasn't even on our staff. The issue was *Imagine – How we can reach the UK* and the writer was Mark Greene. We did it not just because we felt that Mark was asking the right questions, not just because he had analysed the state of Britain and the British Church with incisiveness, but because he was offering the British Church a simple, Biblical and compelling route forward. He pointed out what we still have, not just what we have lost.

The response by our readers was extraordinary. Never before have we received such a wave of positive affirmation from a publication: "wonderful." "Stunning, absolutely brilliant." "Truly inspired of the Lord." "Challenging, encouraging and immensely motivating." Furthermore, it has triggered discussion groups, church strategy meetings, and a series of consultations designed to help the church address the issues he has raised.

Imagine is short but it does exactly what it says on the cover – it helps us all imagine how we can reach our nation. And it shows us how every Christian can be part of it.

Joel Edwards

ONE

This book is about a
possibility...

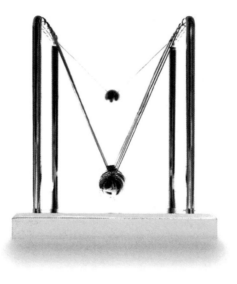

This process should help each of us to see how we can make a difference for Christ, and give us all a clearer idea of how we can work together to make a difference.

This book's primary purpose is to act as a catalyst for a debate. What would help you to make a difference where you are? What would help us to reach the UK? What sort of long-haul strategy is needed for the Christian community to reach out to the nation? Naturally, such a debate has involved leaders from across a variety of different denominations and contexts. But those leaders do need to know what the people of God think. So please complete the questionnaire or offer your contributions on the web at www.licc.org.uk/survey. It is vital that you have your say.

This process should help each of us to see how we can make a difference for Christ, and give us all a clearer idea of how we can work together to make a difference.

we are seeking to reach?

THREE

'*Imagine* there's no heaven,
it's easy if you try,
no hell below us,
above us only sky.'

From 'Imagine' by John Lennon

he UK in a state:
Opportunity Knocks

What is the state of the nation that we are seeking to reach? In December 1999, 'Imagine' was voted the UK's song of the millennium. It seemed, at first glance, to be a surprising choice. After all, most of the people who voted for 'Imagine' were not even alive when it was first released in 1970. Besides, at the dawn of a brand new millennium, wouldn't you expect something more upbeat and celebratory?

Britannia's children, however, were not dancing triumphantly into the new millennium, but tiptoeing in, unsure that we would be able to create a brave new world in which we could, in Lennon's words, 'live as one'. The song had touched a nerve. It probably wasn't Lennon's dream of a God-free, socialist paradise that swung votes. Rather it was the music's gentle, melancholic mood and the general yearning of the lyrics for a better life, a better world, a better tomorrow.

Lennon believed that a world without God would be a happier place. But what the 20th century proved was what Nietzsche predicted: as societies move away from God, they don't get happier, they get unhappier; they don't get more loving, they get more selfish.

The UK is no exception. Christianity has been rejected, and we are not any happier for it. Indeed, after all the myriad of positive changes of the past 40 years, three things are clear:

● The UK has rarely, if ever, been so depressed and directionless.
● The individualistic values that are driving our society are enormously powerful, but they are not delivering the satisfaction people crave.
● A society that can't meet its people's needs is ready to hear good news that might.

The UK has the highest rate of teenage pregnancy in Europe, the highest rate of youth crime, the third highest rate of divorce. We have a growing drug problem and a massive drink problem. And you can't blame unemployment – the UK has one of the lowest rates in Europe. In fact, we work more hours per week than any other European Union nation, and commute the longest. Not surprisingly, this has had a negative impact on the quality of our relationships – with partners, children and friends. We have less time and less energy. The number of days the British economy loses to sickness has doubled in the past seven years, and stress and depression abound. Indeed, prescriptions for anti depressants doubled between 1991 and 2001 from 12 million to 24 million.

Overwork, however, is not the only major factor. Behind these statistics lies the fact that we have lost our sense of national identity and purpose, and this is reflected in the increasing disillusionment with politics. To the public at large, and to the young in particular, none of the major political parties seems to offer any compelling sense of national or individual purpose, or hope. If there is no big idea to bind us together, no grand purpose to pursue, no shared set of values we really agree about, it is hardly a surprise that people become more individualistic and more self-centred, more concerned about their rights and less about their duties.

Prime Minister Tony Blair, speaking in 1995, expressed it thus:

'We enjoy a thousand material advantages over any previous generation, and yet we suffer a depth of insecurity and spiritual doubt they never knew.'

The situation has not improved since then. In the light of its 2002 census, the youth culture magazine *The Face* wrote: 'If identity crisis is a form of madness, then *Young Britain* 2002 is a schizoid manic-depressive with bombsite self-esteem. Our status as the most boozed-up, drug-skewed, pregnancy-prone wasters in Europe is pretty much unchallenged.'

Certainly, our technologies have made us better connected – by car, jet, phone, text and the web – but we are more fragmented. We know more people, but have fewer friends. We lead 'spider lives', as the Henley Centre puts it: we skitter along the threads of our worldwide webs, picking up all kinds of delicacies, but we can't find a place to rest, nor any source of genuine nourishment or intimacy. People today have a million different options to explore, but no strong set of values to help choose which one might be best.

The new opiate

The only thing keeping this show on the road is the brilliance and variety of our leisure options. Entertainment is the opiate of the masses, and we are distracted from reflective thought and radical action by the power, creativity and pervasiveness of our media. Increasingly, our 'hope', what keeps us going, is the expectation of the next episode of EastEnders. And our identity is to be found in the logos on our clothes. Consumerism – the belief that the key to identity and a sense of belonging is to be found in the purchase and the display of material things – is the religion of our time. It is a formidable foe.

The advertising line, 'Life is full of enough embarrassing moments, don't let your mobile be one of them,' is absurd. Nevertheless, the reality is that the 'wrong' mobile can be a profound threat to an individual's sense of self-esteem. As one 12-year-old Christian said to her Christian parents: 'If you don't buy me the right mobile, don't buy me a mobile at all.' Indeed, the highest level of absenteeism in many secondary schools occurs on non-uniform day. The reason is simple: kids who don't have the right gear, don't turn up. They fear ridicule and rejection by their 'friends'.

Despite what Margaret Thatcher once famously said, there *is* such a thing as society, but you need the right products and logos

Logos
are the idols of our times

to belong. Logos are the idols of our time. They rule our hearts, but they do not satisfy them.

Still searching

Interestingly, though most people have turned away from Christianity, they have not, on the whole, consciously replaced it with an alternative set of ideas that gives them a satisfying sense of identity and purpose. Many people are still searching for some kind of spiritual reality, for some centre to their lives. We see this in the experimentation with a whole host of New Age and Eastern practices, and in the increasing interest in witchcraft and the paranormal. 'Mind, Body, Spirit' sections in high-street bookshops are now given more shelf space than 'Religion'.

Though some are still searching, others have given up believing that there is anything out there worth finding. For example, back in 1995, the 18-year-old Emma Forrest wrote this in her Sunday Times column: 'At 18 we are so sophisticated that leaving school doesn't move us. The subconscious fear is not of adulthood, of success or failure, but that nothing else will move me either.' This profound sense of the pointlessness of the search is increasingly common.

Opportunity knocks

So, why might now be a fertile season for the Gospel? Because we are living in a culture that cannot provide an answer to the fundamental questions about meaning and purpose. And a culture that cannot answer its own questions is a culture open to an answer.

Ultimately, of course, we know that all human beings yearn for a restored relationship with God, for a bridge back across the chasm that our sin has hewn. But different societies, in different circumstances, pose different questions.

Can we answer the questions 'Britannia' now poses? ▶

In this directionless culture,
could a life as a Christian have some great purpose?

In this cynical culture, could being a
Christian give me an outlet for my energy, my passion,
my enthusiasm, my yearning to create a different world?

In this spin-driven culture,
is this Christian life really real?

In this high-tech culture, could knowing Jesus
satisfy my yearning for awe, for some taste of the beyond,
some fragrance of the transcendent?

In this abrasive society, could Christian
communities be safe havens to bring my brokenness,
my hurt and my loneliness?

In this glitzy, powerful, in-your-face culture,
could Christ give me the power to live differently?

Imagine a way of life that could offer all that.

Power for life

We know Christianity works. And it works not only because Christ is the truth, but because Christ works in a radically different way to the other major religions. Other religions expect changes in behaviour to lead to a change of heart – they work from the outside in. Christ works from the inside out: 'Therefore, if anyone is in Christ, they are a new creation. The old has passed, the new has come' (2 Corinthians 5:17). We have a new nature and ready access to the Holy Spirit to help us lead the life that Christ calls us to. The Gospel has the power to save, to transform and to sustain.

One way in a multi-faith society

Making the case that Christianity is the only true way is more challenging in a multi-faith, multi-cultural society. Many Christians have lost confidence in the Gospel. We may be able to confess that Jesus is 'my lord' but do we really believe that he is *The* Lord – the only way to the Father?

In reality, the historical, circum-stantial and textual evidence for the life of Christ and His resurrection are entirely robust. Christianity is not only intellectually coherent, but in its understanding of the loving nature of God, the potential of intimacy with Him, and the benefits of salvation in this life and after death, it need fear no comparison with the offerings of any of the major faiths.

Furthermore, it is important to remember that while a Muslim imam will not welcome the conversion of any of his community to Christianity, he understands the claim to exclusive truth. The Koran is clear about the duty to seek the conversion of the 'infidel' and clear about the eternal consequences of not acknowledging Muhammad as Allah's final prophet.

Nevertheless, the liberal humanist establishment jumps to Muslims' defence, as if a more robustly conversionist Christian Church is a threat to social harmony, public order and world peace. Their apparent altruism conceals the truth that the real threat is to their belief – the belief that there is no absolute truth, a creed that brands anyone who claims to know 'The Truth' as arrogant and intolerant.

It is vital to see this. Obviously, Christians should try to reach out to those of other faiths, yet the greatest challenge in the UK is not from other faiths but from the individualistic, consumerist values of our media-driven culture and the de facto atheism that underpins it.

Nevertheless, if the way of Christ is so superior, why haven't we succeeded in communicating it more persuasively?

FOUR

'And *I'd join* the movement,
If there was one I could
believe in.
Yeah, I'd break bread and wine,
If there was a church
I could **receive in**.'

From 'Acrobat', Achtung Baby, by U2

The Church in a state

It's pretty easy to criticise the Church in the UK. In fact, it's so easy, almost everyone does it. The purpose here, however, is not to examine the range of criticisms levelled at the Church, but rather to try to explore the major underlying problems that have inhibited the communication of Christ in the UK. Three points emerge that we will look at in greater depth later.

❶ It is not primarily the world's values that have prevented the Church from reaching out effectively, it is the Church's values.

❷ The problem with Church culture is not that it is irrelevant to those outside the Christian community, but that it is not an authentic expression of the culture of the people in it.

❸ The primary evangelistic problem that the Church faces is not the resistance of those who don't believe the good news about Jesus, but the failure to envision, equip and support those who do.

The effective Church

First, it is important to remember that not all churches are in decline. Church attendance is growing in one in five Anglican dioceses, and Black-majority churches are flourishing.

Second, the church remains an enormous force for good in our country. Indeed, look around many neighbourhoods and ask yourself:

● Who is running drop-in sessions for isolated and often lonely mums?

- Who is running a lunch club for the elderly?

- Who is providing an after-school haven for latchkey kids?

- Who is reaching out to the local home for those with disabilities?

- Who is providing kids' holiday clubs?

- Who is running a homeless centre?

- Who gives most to the poor voluntarily?

The answer is often the people of the local church. No one contributes more to this society voluntarily than local churches and the pastors who lead them. And it is a contribution increasingly recognised by both central and local governments. A Bristol University survey showed that, overall, Christians are three-and-a-half times more likely to do something helpful for someone outside their immediate family than the general population. If 'all you need is love', then, in the neighbourhood at least, love often abounds.

Spitting image?

Nevertheless, the Church in the UK has a terrible image. From the benign but ineffectual Reverend Timms in Postman Pat, to the benign but at least red-blooded Vicar of Dibley, the image of the Church has been ever thus.

The Church would be well advised to pay more attention to its media communications, but the UK will not be won by a series of high-profile advertising campaigns, nor through greater presence on the media, desirable though that is. In the long term, substance matters more than image, and relationships more than TV programmes. Similarly, 'customer satisfaction' is more potent than a slick slogan, and word-of-mouth testimony more powerful than TV commercials.

Alas, many of the Church's current customers are far from satisfied.

The national Church is criticised by its leaders and its members for its poor administration, and for its failure to speak out on major social and economic issues – though it does. It is criticised for its failure to engage with government, the media, the educational establishment – though it does. Nevertheless, it is true that, over the past 20 years, though the Church has spoken, it has rarely had an effective public voice.

The criticism of the Church goes beyond central leadership to its performance at the local level. Here it is criticised for its failure to reach children, teenagers, singles, marrieds, the middle-aged – essentially everyone except the elderly. It is criticised for its failure to address the needs of

Is the church a magnet or a deterrent to the Gospel?

employed women, its failure to attract men, its failure to provide a community of acceptance for non-practising homosexuals, and its flight from the arts. Church structures are criticised for being inflexible, and too hierarchical. Preaching is criticised for its irrelevance to daily life, and worship services in many churches are not merely unattractive to those outside the Church but are often excruciatingly dull to those within it.

These criticisms reflect a deep crisis. And they come not just from perennial whingers or from people disappointed that there are very few hymns with 'hip-hop' arrangements, they come from committed people. And they often come from committed people in churches that are not only full but growing and widely perceived to be successful. In sum, there is a growing concern that the local church is failing to meet the legitimate needs of its members, never mind reaching out to those on the fringe and beyond.

Of course, Christians are not called to preach the Church but to preach Christ and His Gospel. Nevertheless, the state of the institutional Church and of individual church communities often acts either as a magnet or as a deterrent to the Gospel.

Furthermore, the Church, as the community of believers, is meant to play a crucial role in envisioning, equipping and supporting Christians for the life God intended, which includes sharing Christ's love with others.

Three questions emerge:

❶ Does your church effectively help you to live in the contemporary world?

❷ Is your church effective in preparing people for their role in mission?

❸ Is your church an attractive community to those who don't yet know Jesus?

Of course, there are some fine churches that are attractive to non-believers and effective in equipping their people for mission, but broadly speaking most people would answer these questions 'no'.

So what are the key underlying causes for the Church's sagging performance with existing members, and its lack of impact more widely? Let's look first at the issue of Church culture.

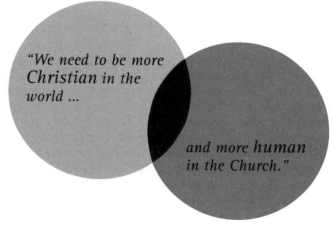

"We need to be more *Christian* in the *world* ...

and more human in the Church."

Brian Draper

FIVE

How many roads did I travel
          before I walked down the one
that led me to you?

From 'Holy', Woven & Spun, by Nicole Norderman

The road to irrelevance, part 1:

The culture block

Most Christians have a very good grasp of UK culture – they live in it. They wake up in the morning, listen to the radio, read newspapers, go to work, are managed, trained and motivated in particular ways, go shopping, play football, watch TV... the Church is in the world day in, day out.

So here's a mystery: why is so much of the way we do things in church alien and off-putting to explorers, when during the week we appear to have so much in common with them?

Perhaps the reason is because we have created a community in which the way things are done does not reflect the culture of the bulk of the people in the Church. We cannot find ways to express ourselves. On the whole, we do not sing songs with tunes that most of our people like. We do not use the language that most people use. We do not address the issues that most people want addressed. We do not give people an opportunity to ask the questions that are really on their minds. We do not create ways of meeting and ways of learning that resonate with the ways of meeting and learning of contemporary life.

The primary problem with Church culture is not just that it is unattractive to people who don't know Jesus. The primary problem is that it is often not an authentic expression of the culture of the people in the Church – it is not even 'our' culture.

Of course, Christian culture should at root be a counter-culture. Christian culture is not intended to mimic any particular society's culture. There ought to be things about Church culture that an explorer finds alien.

But these ought to be things that have their roots in a response to the person of Christ, not in a false belief that 18th century rhythms and 18th century idioms are necessarily closest to godliness.

This is not to say that old songs cannot be sung, that old rites cannot be performed. Indeed, such songs and rites may well resonate with people's desire for a sense of the eternal continuity of the message, or encourage a sense of the transcendent.

Nevertheless, in every generation we need not only to pass on the best of the past, but also to connect to the present and allow new songs, new ways of learning, new ways of relating and new ways of making decisions to find expression.

Whole-loaf discipleship

Furthermore, Church culture has sometimes presented a limited view of what it means to be human – and is often perceived to be without spontaneity, freedom of expression, fun and the enjoyment of the material world. Christ came to give us 'abundant life', and it is each Christian's calling to explore, and help others to explore, the imaginative possibilities of that abundant life in Christ.

Christ's transforming Spirit is intended not only to affect everything we do but all our being – mind, body, emotions, will, spirit – like yeast pervading the whole loaf. Whole-loaf Christianity rejoices in the senses – in the fragrance of a rose, in the liberating joy of moving limbs in sport and dance, in human expression through the arts.

Whole-loaf, whole-life Christianity is honest, open, vulnerable. It does not censor the agony of broken relationships, the bewilderment of unanswered questions, the struggle of work, the scandal of death, the impact of evil on ourselves and those around us. In sum, whole-loaf, whole-life Christianity embraces the wonders and griefs of humanity in all its fullness in God's world.

As LICC's Brian Draper puts it: 'We need to be more Christian in the world, and more human in the Church.'

Too often Church culture looks to be life-denying, not life-affirming. The UK needs both to hear the message of Christ and to see the power of Christ working itself out in the authenticity of people's lives.

If we create an overall Church culture that is relevant and genuinely enriching for our own people, we will create a culture that will be much more relevant to many who don't yet know Christ. And we will give our own people the joy and confidence that knowing Christ really does make a difference.

Christ came to give us *'abundant life'*, and it is each Christian's calling to *explore*, and help others to explore, the imaginative *possibilities* of that abundant life in Christ.

SIX

"Well, I *never pray*.

But tonight I'm

on my knees, *yeah*.

*I need to hear some sounds that
recognise the **pain** in me*"

From 'Bittersweet Symphony' by The Verve

The road to irrelevance, part 2:

The great divide

Traditional analyses of why the Church has failed to make an impact in the public sphere have tended to focus on a whole host of external factors – ideological, technological and economic. All these factors are said to have combined in the post-war period to relegate faith – all faiths – to the private sphere. Faith was reduced to a matter for personal, private reflection. It was put in a compartment. It had no place in the public arena, whether that be in work, school or politics. Faith ceased to be the central organising principle that informed all of life and all of life's decisions and actions.

The problem with blaming social forces for the decline of Christianity is that it presumes that Christian doctrines and lifestyle have no power to resist their onslaught. In other words, we blame the world for the demise of Christian values, and perhaps don't ask ourselves to what extent we might be responsible. To paraphrase John Stott, you can't blame the meat for going rotten – that's what meat does. You blame the salt for not being there to preserve it.

Privatising Christianity

The primary reason Christianity has had little impact on the public sphere is not because the world has privatised the Gospel, but because we have.

Research reveals that 47 per cent of church attendees say that the teaching they receive in their churches is irrelevant to their daily lives. When you probe more deeply into where church teaching is helpful, you discover that church teaching is least helpful when it comes to where people spend most time – home and work.

> ### Helpfulness rating by life area
>
> *(on a scale of 0-4, from least to most helpful)*
>
> | | |
> |---|---|
> | Personal | 2.57 |
> | Church | 2.12 |
> | Home | 1.83 |
> | Work/school | 1.68 |

Importantly, few people said that the problem with preaching and teaching was the preacher's delivery or communication skills or even their failure to engage with the Bible (though this remains a concern). The core issue was the relevance of the material to people's lives. The problem is not primarily one of form but of content.

Overall, churchgoers are not looking to be entertained, they are looking for wisdom for their daily lives. They want to know how to live Christianly. And that is not being delivered.

This is not just a pity for them, but it is a tragedy evangelistically because millions of people in the UK are thirsting for practical wisdom for living. People may not be directly interested in the Gospel, but many are interested in how to choose a career, a partner, have a happier marriage, bring up children and manage debt.

This failure to deliver wisdom for daily living applies to some of the finest teaching churches in Britain. One member of such a congregation said: 'The teaching is excellent. It's just very hard to apply it to my life.'

Research shows that this failure to make the connection between the Word of God and the world manifests itself right across the denominations.

Private irrelevance

The drop in the perceived relevance of church teaching to daily life is paralleled by a drop in private prayer and daily Bible reading. Not surprisingly, perhaps. After all, if my trained pastor can't show me how this 8th century BC text applies to my 21st century AD life, what chance have I got? In sum, Christians spend less time in focused reflection on God and less time with people who share their worldview and their concerns.

Prayer, biblical reflection and meeting purposefully with God's people are not the only ways to sustain a relationship with God, but they are not simply traditional methods, they are biblical methods. Of course, people often say that it's a matter of time: certainly more of us are working outside the home, and more of us are working harder and commuting further. But we still have time.

Nor has Bible reading declined simply because reading has declined. People, particularly the middle classes, still read significant amounts. And they certainly read what's important to them. Bible reading has declined because we are not convinced that God has something essential and exhilarating to say to us about how to live in His world. And prayer has declined because we are not convinced that it will make any difference to our daily lives.

We will not grow more effective for God unless we grow more attentive to God. And we will not grow attentive to God unless we are convinced that listening makes a difference. Ask yourself two questions:

❶ Do I understand the relevance of Christianity to my ordinary daily life?

❷ Do I seek God's wisdom and support in my ordinary daily life?

For many Christians in Britain, the answer is likely to be 'no'. We may be convinced that Christ makes a difference to our eternal destination, but does He make a difference to us in our day-to-day decisions?

So, even before we get to the question of whether the Church is equipping its people to share the Gospel, we run headlong into the reality that many Christians simply do not see the compelling relevance of Christianity to their 'ordinary' Christian lives. Why?

The great divide

It is certainly not that our leaders don't care about us, nor that they are incompetent. The key cause is the impact of the sacred-secular divide on virtually every aspect of church life.

The sacred-secular divide involves the pervasive belief that some parts of life are not really important to God – work, school, sport, TV – but anything to do with prayers, church services and church-based activities is.

It is because of the sacred-secular divide that the vast majority of Christians in every denomination feel that they get no significant support for their work from the teaching, prayer, worship, pastoral or community aspects of church life. It is because of the sacred-secular divide that over 50 per cent of them have never heard a sermon on work – something that they will spend around 65 per cent of their waking lives doing for about 40 years. Quotations like this abound: 'I teach in Sunday school 45 minutes a week and they haul me up to the front and the whole church prays for me. I teach in school 40 hours a week and no one ever prays for me.'

That's the sacred-secular divide: praying for one part of a Christian's life but not another; believing that teaching in Sunday school for 45 minutes a week is more important to God than teaching in school for 40 hours a week.

It is because of the sacred-secular divide that the Harry Potter novels have been so widely commented on by Christian leaders, but the choice of literature for the national curriculum has been almost entirely ignored. The primary reason the Church has engaged so vigorously with the Harry Potter books is because of their setting in a school for wizards and witches – the setting raises issues about the 'spiritual' realm of the occult, a realm the Church quite rightly feels it should engage in.

The sacred – secular divide, which keeps our day-to-day lives separate from our church lives, has led to flawed theologies of church and outreach.

Meanwhile, back in the national curriculum, kids are reading all kinds of often very fine literature: Samuel Becket's *Waiting for Godot* or DH Lawrence's *Sons and Lovers*, for example. And they are not just reading them, they're studying them hard, learning quotations, writing essays. Quite rightly. But are the children of today's Church being equipped to use a biblical perspective to respond to Becket's atheism or Lawrence's view of free love? Are they being equipped to respond biblically to any other aspect of their curriculum?

> *The question is not 'How can I use this person in the local church?' but 'How does God want to develop and use this person?'*

To date, we, at LICC, after considerable research, have not yet been able to identify a single resource for youth workers that encourages them to help their young people think biblically about their studies at school. The result is that, by default, our kids learn very young that the 9-to-5 is not important to God. We have a leisure-time Christianity.

Leisure-time Christianity

This continues on into university education. Norman Fraser, formerly a senior executive with Universities and Colleges Christian Fellowship (UCCF), the UK's largest student ministry, lamented: 'I could practically guarantee that you could go into any Christian Union in Britain and not find a single student who could give you a biblical perspective on the subject they are studying to degree level.'

That's the sacred-secular divide – not expecting Christians to think Christianly about what they're doing in the world.

The sacred-secular divide has promoted a leisure-time Christianity, not a 24/7, whole-life Christianity. Evenings and Sundays are God's, 9-to-5 is the world's. And so the sacred-secular divide leads adults to believe that really holy people become missionaries, moderately holy people become ministers, and people who are not much use to God get a job. Bah humbug.

God is the God of all of life

Christ claims all of our lives – our life at work and our life in the neighbourhood. If we want to see the UK won for Christ, the sacred-secular divide must be expunged from every thought and prayer. After all, most of our interactions with the 90 per cent of people who don't know Jesus occur on the 'secular' side of the great divide – the side that we and our communities rarely pray for, or consider vital to God.

The sacred-secular divide is pervasive and has contributed to flawed theologies of the Church, of the role of the minister and of outreach.

Flawed view of the Church

In Matthew 5, Jesus gives the disciples two similes to describe the people of God, the Church: the light on a hill, and salt. Here light is primarily an image of the Church gathered together. What does the community of Christ look like to the watching world? If we love one another, John records, all people will know that we are Jesus' disciples. The loving relationships between Christians are a testimony to the world of the transforming power of the One we follow.

Second, the people of God are compared to salt scattered in the world. This is a call to individual Christians to work out their faithfulness in the world. But does the individual Christian cease to be a member of the Church when they are out in the world? Not according to the Bible.

In reality, however, the average Christian does not feel that they go to work as the individual representative of the body of Christ, supported in prayer and fellowship by other Christians. No, the average Christian believes they go to work alone.

The impact of the sacred-secular divide has been to see the 'church gathered' as more important to mission than the 'church scattered'. Indeed, the vast majority of church evangelistic initiatives have tended to be domestically focused and pastor-centred. The goal becomes to get non-believers into a domestic or church context to listen to a pastor, live or on video, as opposed to get the non-believer into relationship with Christ through a relationship with a Christian. We spend an enormous amount of energy trying to work out how to make the church a place people will want to come to, and little energy working out how we can train Christians to make the most of the places they already go to.

Flawed view of the pastor's role

The sacred-secular divide also manifests itself in a flawed understanding of the role of the pastor. In Ephesians 4:11-12, Paul writes: 'It was He who gave some to be apostles, some to be prophets, some to be evangelists and some to be pastors and teachers, to prepare God's people for works of service, so that the body of Christ may be built up.'

The job of the pastor is to prepare his or her people for their ministry – which is likely to involve contexts outside a one-mile, or even three-mile, radius of the local church. Indeed, if we think not so much about where people are at 11 o'clock on Sunday morning, but where they are at 11 o'clock on Monday morning, then we will, in almost every case, get a much clearer picture of their potential for mission. The question is not 'How can I use this person in the local church?' but 'How does God want to develop and use this person?'

Unfortunately, very few pastors see their role in this way – otherwise they would have been equipping their people to be effective for Christ in work and school. The sacred-secular divide has, therefore, profoundly affected who does evangelism, in what contexts and in what ways.

The key to mission is to equip Christians for where they are, not where they are not; for where they have relationships, not where they don't.

➡

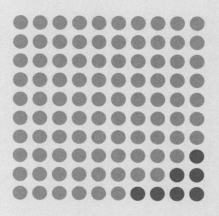

We think that the church is marginalized, in the corner ...

but Monday to Saturday the people of God are in fact out in the world, relating to scores of people.

SEVEN

Never forget that our
greatest assets
walk out of the elevator
at the end of every day.

Advertising guru David Ogilvy of Ogilvy and Mather

Re-invigorating the people of God

This view of the potential of every Christian to serve God where they are is not just a missionary tactic, it is a scriptural truth. It not only has the potential to see many people come to Christ, it has the potential to re-invigorate Christians.

At the moment, many Christians are totally unaware of their potential to serve God where they are. They go to work, do a good job, try to be honest and dash home at the end of the day to go to the prayer meeting or to involve themselves in some church activity, so that they can 'do something for God' that day. They do not know that they have already served God. They do not know that whatever they do can be done to the glory of God.

One woman I met put it this way: 'I've worked in the NHS for 17 years. And for many years I've wondered what ministry God had for me. About a year ago, I suddenly realised where God wanted me: right here in the NHS. And it has transformed my attitude to my job. How sad it is that some people die without realising the ministry God had for them.'

Furthermore if Christ isn't relevant to Christians where we spend most of our time, why should He be relevant to non-Christians where they spend most of their time? And if God isn't relevant to us where we spend most of our time, why would He be relevant where we spend less of our time?

Furthermore, if we Christians don't live as if faith affects all of our life, then why should non-Christians believe that Christianity is relevant to all of theirs? If explorers don't see any difference about us in our work time, then they will continue to believe that Christian activities are merely our preferred way of spending our leisure time – rather than the power plant of our entire existence.

Transform where you are

In addition, the realisation that every Christian can make a difference where they are opens up the possibility not only of modelling the Christian way but of bringing the wisdom of Christ to bear on the way that things are done – in a school, hospital or business. Will the priorities of the King who created all have some impact on His created order? On what products we make, what games we play, what wages we pay, what hours we expect others

We have the people.

And we have them in place. How can we unleash this fantastic resource?

to work and so on. The Christian in God's world has a mandate not only for verbal witness but also for social transformation.

Tragically, the 1945 document was ignored, perhaps because it would have involved such a radical change in the whole focus of church ministry. Or perhaps because, as one commentator put it, the leadership put the Church before the Church's mission, put the institution before the institution's purpose. It is a powerful temptation. The Church that puts the institution before its purpose is as likely to be fruitful as a dance studio that spends all its money and time on the décor and sound quality, rather than teaching people to dance.

The people of God represent a fantastic resource. And it is the failure to unleash that resource that is one of the Church's key problems. As management guru Richard Farson wrote: 'The real strength of a leader is the ability to elicit the strength of the group.'

How can we elicit the strength that is in the Christian community?

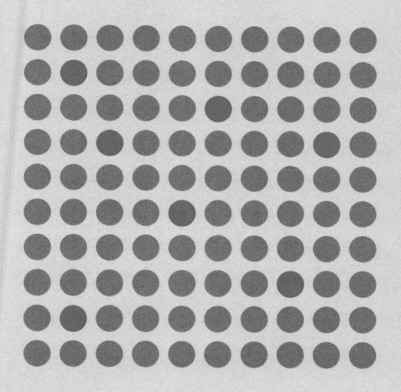

Who do you know already?
What support do you need from your
church to help you minister to them?

EIGHT

We would stand and *respond*
and examine and include and allow
and *forgive* and enjoy and
evolve and discern and inquire
and accept and admit and
divulge and open
and reach out and speak up.

This is my *utopia*,
this is my ideal, my end in sight.

From 'Utopia', Under Rug Swept, by Alanis Morissette

Let my people go

How can the Church create Christian communities that help release the strength of the people where they are? ❶ Ask the people. ❷ Take their responses seriously. Of course, leaders must set the overall direction, but good leaders also seek to find out what issues their people face, and what resources they need to face them. We must listen not only to the Word and the world – double listening, as John Stott called it – but also to God's people – triple listening.

This is not teacher-centred thinking but disciple-centred thinking. Such thinking does not begin with the question: 'How do I tell you what I know?' It begins by asking a question like: 'How can I help you live for Christ where you are?' Or more specific questions like:

- What issues are you facing in your life?
- What is God calling you to do?
- What knowledge do you feel you lack?
- What skills do you need to acquire?
- What questions are you or your non-Christian friends asking?
- What resources would help you?
- What support do you need from your church?

What might we discover?

We might discover that many of us are struggling to integrate faith and life, to integrate faith and work. We might discover that we have a number of unresolved questions ourselves, and that we don't feel confident to answer the questions we imagine non-believers might ask us.

We might discover that in many areas we are thirsting for wisdom to lead our lives – to choose a career, a life-partner, to stay married, to bring up our kids, to manage our finances.

We might discover that many of us feel guilty about our self-perceived failure to make a difference, and that many of us don't really know how to share our faith, and that we are suspicious of formulaic methods.

We might discover that the number one barrier that most Christians feel prevents them from fulfilling their potential in Christ in mission and ministry is fear – fear of their own ignorance, fear for their own self-esteem, fear of being embarrassed, fear of failure, fear of letting God down.

This doesn't let any of us off the hook from seeking to share Christ. We know He expects His people to witness to Him: 'But you will receive power when the Holy Spirit comes on you; and you will be my witnesses in Jerusalem, and in all Judea and Samaria, and to the ends of the earth' (Acts 1:8).

Nevertheless, the contemporary understanding of the concept of witnessing militates against most people ever doing it. A witness is not necessarily a preacher or a debater. A witness is someone who tells others what they have seen and experienced.

You do not need special training to tell someone about the day you met the love of your life. You do not need coaching to tell someone about the squash club you really enjoy. Their response might well be to tell you that their squash club is better, or that they don't like squash because it is the preserve of the middle-class toff, or that tennis is a much better game ... but you can still tell them why you like your squash club.

The power of conversation

Witness is not about winning an argument, but about having a conversation. And the great lack in the contemporary Christian community is not for a new generation of platform evangelists but for a community of people who will talk about Jesus over a cup of coffee.

If the model of witness is an evangelistic sermon or the debating skills of the professional apologist, no wonder people don't speak about Christ. The set-piece, prepared talk is not something you can usually deploy in a pub, and a Gospel tract is a useful tool, but there is a time and a place.

Christianity might have begun to spread through the ancient world through Peter's sermon to a large audience, but it didn't

Is your church making **disciples?** *Are you closer to* **Christ** *than you were a year ago?*

continue that way. Indeed, we have record of very few such addresses to large audiences. Most meetings were in homes far too small to contain the average contemporary British congregation. And most 'preaching' would have born little resemblance to the kind of uninterruptible, monological address we are used to.

Nor did the Gospel spread through tracts or mass media or through the penetration of power structures and channels of influence. It spread through purposeful conversations, underpinned by prayer, empowered by the Holy Spirit and validated by the evidence of changed lives.

However, even if witness is akin to conversation, it is not a 'natural' activity. Speaking about Christ needs to be a spiritually empowered activity. In the Book of Acts, seven times the disciples pray for boldness (NIV), or better translated, 'freedom' to speak about Christ. No doubt they prayed more often. Christian witness cannot be reduced to a technique. It is more than mere conversation, and it is not risk-free. After all, many contemporary people have imbibed relativism and are more likely to respond to even the most direct presentation by saying 'cool', and going on to tell you how crystals have changed their life.

If witness is at its simplest a conversation, this is not to say that we do not have a responsibility to be prepared to answer people's questions. Peter calls on all Christians to 'always be prepared to give an answer to everyone who asks you to give a reason for the hope that you have' (1 Peter 3:15). This former fisherman doesn't tell us that we have to be able to take on the professor of Buddhism at Cambridge, but he does encourage us to be ready with a reason for the hope that we have. (Peter 3:15) We don't have to win the argument, we simply have to state our case.

However, the vast majority of people in our churches are not trained for the mission God has called them to. And there is little point in constant exhortations to ministry and witness if such exhortations are not preceded by appropriate training and accompanied by appropriate support. Tools like *Alpha* and *Christianity Explored* are powerful not just because they allow interested people to explore the Christian faith, but because they give believers the opportunity to clarify theirs. And that leads to much greater confidence.

There are things our people
need to learn.
It's time they were taught.

NINE

Go, therefore, and
make disciples
of all nations, baptising them
in the name of the Father, and of
the Son and of the Holy Spirit,
and *teaching them* to obey
everything I have commanded you.

Jesus of Nazareth, Matthew 28:19-20

Learning to live,
living to learn

The Church's goal is not to build the Church. Christ does that. The goal is to make disciples. That's what Jesus spent most of His time doing in His three years of public ministry. That's what Barnabas did with Paul and John Mark, and Paul with Timothy. Certainly, Jesus spoke to thousands but His focus was on 12. Christ made disciples and commanded us to do the same.

The Church in the UK has a 'convert and retain' strategy. Christ had a 'disciple and release' strategy. Are we making disciples?

Disciple-making is altogether messier than preaching and teaching. You can use big meetings and programmes to help make disciples, but programmes are not enough. The disciple-maker has to get into close relationship with the disciple, has to be in a position to ask sharp questions, to hold up the mirror of God's Word, to deal with the particular pressures and temptations that the individual has. Consider these questions:

❶ Is your church making disciples?
❷ Are you closer to Christ than you were a year ago?
❸ In the last year, have you learned a significant amount about what it means to live as a follower of Christ in the contemporary world?

Most pastors have been trained to teach and preach and counsel. Disciple-making, however, is more than that, and most pastors have not been trained in the art of disciple-making. Generally pastors are not members of a home group or involved in mentoring relationships with anyone in their churches. Nor do the structures in most churches lend themselves to disciple-making. In fact, pastors spend very little time on disciple-making or passing on

A disciple is an *active, intentional learner.*

A disciple is an apprentice and a **practitioner** – not just a student of the Word but a doer of it.

A disciple is a **follower** of a particular teacher.

A disciple is **accountable** to someone who knows them and helps them to learn and grow and live.

A disciple is **outwardly** orientated, focused on **helping others** learn what it means to be a *disciple.*

the skills of disciple-making. They spend most time on administration, crisis counselling and visiting, preparing and leading services, and sermon preparation.

The average pastor has a job description that virtually no one in their congregation would accept. The average pastor is also, according to Evangelical Alliance research, overworked, over-stressed and poorly paid. Many are thinking about leaving their job.

The average pastor is also gifted, committed to Christ and committed to their people. We can't ask them to do any more. But we must release them to do what's really important.

Focusing on the few

Jesus focused on the development of a small group of people. Do we?

A pastor who gets involved in disciple-making will discover countless benefits for the wider congregation. They will develop relationships that reveal the real issues on people's hearts, uncover the questions that Christians face in the world, see where they fail and succeed, and discern why. It is from such in-depth, purposeful relationships with the few that the many are often best served.

We might ask ourselves: Have we made any disciples lately? Is our teaching building up outwardly orientated disciples or just retaining converts? Do our services contribute to building up disciples or do they simply help maintain faith? Do we have leaders willing to pursue a training agenda? Or a deep enough conviction that communicating the Good News is central to discipleship?

Lifelong learning

Furthermore, do our church patterns reflect the New Testament's four-fold focus on prayer, learning, relationships and communion? 'They devoted themselves to prayer, to the apostles' teaching, to fellowship and the breaking of bread' (Acts 2:42).

The Church of Christ is not intended to be a community where teaching 'happens', it is intended to be a community that is 'devoted to teaching'. It is intended to be a learning organisation. Most churches aren't, and never will be, as long as there is an overwhelming emphasis on the Sunday service.

You can do a lot of things in an hour or 90 minutes on a Sunday, but you can't do everything. We simply cannot expect any pastor/teacher, however gifted, to teach the whole Bible, all the major Christian doctrines, what to think about cloning, abortion, Iraq, EastEnders, REM, how to be a better husband/wife/friend/colleague/boss/parent, and how to have a greater impact in the community, the local school, the workplace – in 10 minutes or even 30 minutes on a Sunday. And you certainly can't give everyone an opportunity to ask questions about the teaching they've had or explore their doubts.

There is nothing wrong with monological preaching. But it is most effective in contexts where it is combined with other means of learning. We need more teaching, not less – particularly because contemporary people who come to church have learned less at school or at home about Christianity than people of previous generations. It can't all be done on a Sunday, nor should any minister pretend it can be. Most people need to be prepared to devote themselves to active learning, as opposed to expecting to grow strong on titbits.

Three-tier learning

Of course, different Church streams will respond to the need differently. Much of this has already been explored by the cell church movement and by the G12 cell model, and there is an enormous amount to learn from what they are learning. However, the issue is not about any particular form that the response takes, but the content we seek to deliver and the outcomes we hope to achieve. That said, a mainstream Protestant church with a Sunday service might operate with a three-tier structure, offering:

❶ The opportunity to worship God in the community of believers and hear the Bible taught.

❷ The opportunity to explore the truths of the Bible in a context where questions can be asked and truths applied to contemporary life (eg home groups, adult Sunday school and midweek teaching).

❸ The opportunity to develop intimate, mutually supportive relationships of accountability and service with a small number of people in which there is the freedom to ask and answer tough questions (eg modified home groups, prayer partnerships, commuter groups on the train, workplace triplets, pre-clubbing sessions).

Essentially this was the pattern that the great Methodist evangelist and church-planter John Wesley developed. But the key is not the form he used in his era, but rather for us to be imaginative about how we work with the rhythms of contemporary life to help one another grow in discipleship.

Interestingly, many leaders argue that people just won't come to demanding activities. But that partly depends on whether we mean 50 per cent of a congregation or a group of disciples. Many people will give an evening to a learning activity – and do. What can we do with the time people will give?

We must not allow the search for great models to prevent us from starting the process of making disciples

For example, in-depth Bible studies such as *Precept* and *Bible Study Fellowship* are growing in popularity. The reason for this is simple: you study the Bible in depth, with life application in mind, and it helps you to lead your life. Busy commuter-belt professionals will give hours to something that delivers, but resent every second spent in an anodyne, flaky group. This isn't to say that the future lies in high-commitment, in-depth Bible studies, but it is to say that part of the future lies in creating contexts in which people are taught and learn how to live for Christ today. And it is vital that this is done in contexts where questions can be asked, doubts expressed, disagreements voiced, difficulties wrestled with and commitments supported.

Until the advent of cell church, the primary solution in the UK to the limitations of monological Sunday preaching was to start home groups. But research has suggested that over 70 per cent of home groups had no conscious goals at all. Of those that did, half of them were not actually goals but lists of activities. That is, the group got together to do things – some combination of study, prayer, worship, friendship – but without any idea of specific outcomes, eg to grow in particular ways, to learn particular skills or to encourage one another in specific kinds of ways.

Furthermore, the tendency was to impose the same set of material on every group, as if it were really the case that one size fits all. This makes very little sense from a training and learning perspective because it fails to recognise that people may be at different stages in their Christian development and at different stages in their lives, and therefore have very different needs. One size fits one.

Disciples not only need a place to learn, they need a place to be 'real', to allow the sharing of questions and intimate discoveries, struggles and joys, temptations and failures, sins and triumphs. In sum, they need relationships of support and accountability. This can be achieved in a whole variety of ways – in triplets, in pairs, in cells – but such relationships are for many people one of the most important keys to continued growth in Christ.

Better to start somewhere

If we are to create communities that have disciple-making on their hearts, it will probably require our leaders to learn new skills. Just as we seek to create life-long learning among our people, so we should take the life-long learning of our pastors seriously.

Sadly, pastoral ministry is almost the only profession left where people seriously expect someone to learn pretty much all they need to learn for a lifetime in two or three years. We don't expect that of a lawyer, an accountant or a doctor. And it is an issue that every church needs to take seriously. How can we ensure our pastors are learning what they need to learn? What's in our budget for that?

Pastors may well ask: How indeed do we make disciples today? How can we create congregations that are disciple-making in orientation?

The answer is probably to start small and slow. No pastor can do all the work of disciple-making, but a pastor can begin somewhere and train those who will be able to share the load. Vitally, this will in time spread the sources of wisdom across the community. Otherwise, the church runs the danger of becoming far too dependent on the professional pastoral team. They can't do it all, and even if they could, they're not meant to.

We have much to learn, and trumpeting some new programme as the solution to the Church's woes will probably be met with the scepticism it deserves. Nevertheless, there are a number of resources available. Furthermore, there may well be new models already being tried that will come to light through the process that the LICC and Evangelical Alliance are leading.

Yes, we have much to learn, but we must not allow the search for 'great models' to inhibit starting the process of making disciples. A leader could do worse than simply asking their congregation what would help them, or beginning a group with a small number of people with the express intent of helping them to grow.

The Church's greatest resource is the people we already have. We must find ways to help them go to those who don't know Christ – with generosity, humility and purpose.

Imagine if we all asked *Jesus* the question:

Lord, how can I make a difference for you today?

T E N

Your country needs you

The UK is a post-Christian country and our families, friends, neighbours and co-workers need to hear the Gospel in terms they can understand. We cannot expect them to come to our church buildings, they must learn about Christ from us.

My conviction is this:

> **The UK will never be converted until we create open, authentic, learning and praying communities that are focused on making whole-life disciples who take the opportunities to show and share the Gospel wherever they relate to people in their daily lives.**

And we must pray.

Every Christian has this high calling: to be involved in the unfolding history of God's relationship with humankind.

Every Christian can be different where they are and make a difference where they are.

And every one of us is involved in the struggle to overcome evil with good, to support the weak, to comfort the bereaved, to feed the poor, to create a country, a town, a workplace, a school, a home where the yeast of the Kingdom transforms all.

Let us pray.

Imagine if we created praying, supportive, learning communities that helped us to grow in wisdom, in humanity and in generous love – communities that people wanted to come to. And communities that enabled their people to go to others.

Imagine if we all asked Jesus the question:

'Lord, how can I make a difference for you today?'

What difference would that make? Where might Jesus take us, individually and together? A very exciting place, which, in many cases, will be exactly where we already are. But it will look different as we begin to see it through His eyes. And even more different as He begins to work in it.

May it be so wherever you are. And in our land.

To comment on *Imagine* or contribute to the research go to www.licc.org.uk/survey